D1178828

EXPLORING MATERIALS

Building Materials

Malcolm Dixon

EXPLORING MATERIALS

Building Materials
Materials in the Environment
Materials in your Home
Materials on the Move

751, 168/J691

Editor: Joanna Housley
Designer: John Christopher

First published in 1993 by Wayland (Publishers) Limited,
61 Western Road, Hove, East Sussex, BN3 1JD, England

British Library Cataloguing in Publication Data
Dixon, Malcolm
  Building Materials. – (Exploring Materials Series)
  I. Title II. Series
  691

ISBN 0 7502 0702 7

Typeset by Strong Silent Type
Printed and bound in Spain by Graficas Estella.

For Michelle and Joanne

Picture acknowledgements

The publishers wish to thank the following for supplying the photographs in this book: Chapel Studios 26, 29, 38, 39; Eye Ubiquitous 41 (John Northover), 42; Photri 19 (Macdonald Photography); Tony Stone Worldwide 4 (Marcus Brooke), 5 (Vic Thomasson), 6 (Suzanne & Nick Geary), 8 (John Bassett), 10 (Glen Allison), 11, 12 (Doug Armand)), 17, 21 (Dave Saunders), 24 (top, Peter Poulides), (below, David Bassett), 27 (right, David Hanson), (left, Geoff Johnson), 28,34 (Tony Craddock), 36, 44; Topham Picture Source 37; Wayland Picture Library 9, 16, 35 (top); ZEFA 35 (below). Artwork by Peter Bull.

NOTES FOR PARENTS AND TEACHERS

Teachers will find this book useful in implementing the National Curriculum (Science) at Key Stages 1, 2 and 3. Within BUILDING MATERIALS there is information and activities which are particularly relevant to Attainment Targets 1 (Scientific Investigation) and 3 (Materials and their properties). BUILDING MATERIALS can, of course, be developed as a cross-curricular topic involving science, technology, geography, history, mathematics and English.

There are some activities in this book which will require the help of a parent or teacher. The section on places to visit will be useful to parents during weekends and school holidays.

Contents

Materials and building

Throughout history men and women have used various materials to build homes, bridges and other structures. The materials used by early nomadic people were those provided by nature — stones, trees and animal skins. People discovered later that stronger homes could be made using mud, clay and grass. These materials are still used in some countries with hot, dry climates. In our modern world we can find examples of very old and grand structures erected by the Egyptians, Romans, Greeks and Chinese. We can also see many houses, palaces and cathedrals which were built hundreds of years ago.

BELOW
These school buildings in Ethiopia are made from local materials.

ABOVE
The Parthenon, a great marble temple built in 440 BC, overlooks the city of Athens, Greece.

We can compare the materials used to build the structures of the past with the materials we use for building today.

New manufactured materials, such as steel and concrete, mean that very high structures, and bridges which cross great distances, can be built. Plastics are being used more as building materials. It has been suggested that new and stronger materials will be developed in the future to replace steel and concrete in some building work.

Builders, engineers and architects have to decide which material is the best for a particular job. They need to consider the properties of the material, how much it costs and whether it is easily available. They also have to listen to the needs and wishes of the people for whom the building is being constructed.

Iron, steel and other metals

Most metals are taken out of ores found in the ground. Some metals have special properties which make them excellent materials to use in construction. They can be hammered into sheets or bent and changed into different shapes without breaking. They are often strong and heavy. They conduct electricity and heat, do not melt easily and are ductile (can be drawn out into wire).

BELOW
The Eiffel Tower in Paris is a famous iron structure. In 1889 it was the world's tallest building.

Although metals have been used for over 5,000 years, it was not until 1779 that iron was used to build a bridge. This bridge, with a span of 35 m across the River Severn at Ironbridge in England, still stands today. Nearly 400 tonnes of a type of iron known as cast iron, containing a small amount of carbon (about 4%), was used. The construction of this bridge led to much greater use of iron as a building material.

Molten iron is now produced in blast furnaces. Iron ores, such as haematite, magnetite and limonite, are mixed with coke and heated to form a material called sinter. Coke, iron ore, sinter and limestone are fed into the top of the blast furnace. Hot air is blasted in through nozzles, producing intense heat in the furnace. The iron in the iron ore and sinter melts and runs down to the bottom of the furnace. This iron, called pig iron, is removed at regular intervals. Over 800 million tonnes of iron are produced throughout the world every year.

ABOVE Pig iron is produced at an extremely high temperature in a blast furnace.

Steel is the most important metal in use today. It is widely used in building and in almost every modern industry. Without steel we would be unable to make the machines we use to produce other materials, such as glass, plastic and concrete, which are vital in modern building methods.

RIGHT
Many buildings have
frameworks made from steel.

The various types of steel are alloys that are formed from iron and other materials. Mild steel, used to make girders, is an alloy of iron and a small amount (less than 0.5%) of the non-metal carbon. Stainless steel, used to make things which must not rust, is often made from iron, chromium (18%) and nickel (8%). Stainless steel, although expensive, has become popular as a maintenance-free exterior cladding for buildings.

Pig iron or steel scrap or a mixture of both, depending on the type of steel required, is the basic material needed to make steel.

A steel-making method called the Basic Oxygen System is used to make most of the steels used in building today. A modern steel furnace can convert up to 400 tonnes of basic materials into steel within forty minutes. When special steels are needed a different process, an Electric Arc Furnace, is used. This method allows the steel manufacturers to use cold scrap steel to produce steels with special properties. Further processing of the molten steel is needed before it can be used in such shapes as tubes, sheets or bars.

Steel is used for the foundations of buildings and in producing reinforced and pre-stressed concrete. The great strength of steel has allowed engineers to design and build bridges to span long distances and buildings of enormous heights.

The Forth Railway Bridge in Scotland was completed in 1889. It was constructed using 60,000 tonnes of steel and was the first bridge to be built using steel on such a large scale. The Sydney Harbour Bridge, spanning 503 m across Australia's busiest harbour, was completed in 1931. It was one of the first examples of steel arch bridges to have railway and road decks suspended from a massive arch. To test for any faults in the finished structure, 72 locomotives, each with a mass of 7,600 tonnes, were used.

BELOW The Sydney Harbour Bridge in Australia has a steel arch supported by granite towers.

RIGHT
The Golden Gate Bridge
in San Francisco, USA.
You can see how the
roadway is suspended from
the massive steel cables.

The Golden Gate Bridge in San Francisco, USA is one of the most famous suspension bridges in the world. Completed in 1937, it stretches across 1,280 m. For nearly thirty years this was the longest distance spanned by any bridge. The Humber Bridge in England was finished in 1981 after nine years' work. It spans a distance of 1,410 m and is constructed from steel and reinforced concrete. The main deck of the bridge is hung from two massive steel cables which are fixed into concrete on the river banks. These support cables run across the tops of two 200 m-high reinforced concrete towers. The cables themselves are made up of many strands of steel wire. The bridge's huge road deck was constructed from hollow steel boxes. This decking is suspended from the two main cables by steel wires called hangers. A road surface of mastic asphalt covers the steel decking and prevents water getting through to the steel.

Many skyscrapers have been built using steel frameworks. These frameworks, which are constructed using steel beams joined by rivets, bolts or by welding, then have the floors and wall panels fitted to them. The Manhattan area of New York has many skyscrapers that have been built using this method. One of the most famous, the Empire State Building, was built within eighteen months during 1930 and 1931, and yet it has 102 storeys, reaching 420 m high. Some modern buildings are designed to show the framework which supports the building. The Hong Kong and Shanghai Bank, completed in 1985, has the floors hanging from eight steel columns, each 200 m tall. The building is covered in aluminium and thick glass panels but the steel frame is clearly visible from outside the building.

BELOW
Steel has been used to build great structures which have changed our lives. Enormous oil rigs made with steel have enabled us to search beneath the seas of the world.

Aluminium is a valuable metal which is used in building mainly because it is so light. When combined with other metals such as manganese or copper it becomes much stronger. Aluminium and its alloys are widely used as roofing materials, for window frames, double-glazed doors and tubing.

Lead is a metal with many different properties. It is heavy, soft and melts and bends easily. It has been widely used as a roofing material and in domestic plumbing. However, since the effects of lead poisoning have been understood, lead pipes have been replaced by plastic and copper.

BELOW
The steel frame of the Hong Kong and Shanghai Bank in Hong Kong can be seen from outside the building.

Build a tower and a bridge

YOU WILL NEED

some paper fasteners
a hole punch
some sheets of thin card
an object with a mass of 100 g
an object with a mass of 200 g
scissors

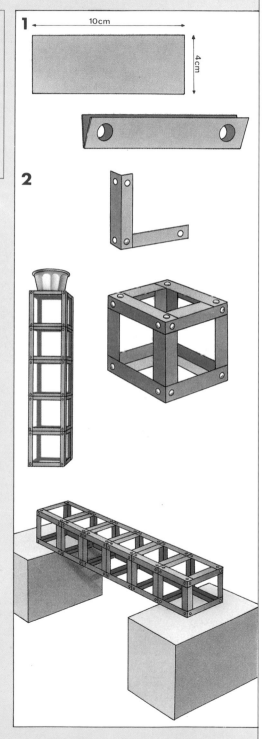

1. Cut strips of card each measuring 10 cm by 4 cm. Fold the card strips as shown. Punch holes at both ends of the strips.

2. Use a paper fastener to fix two of your card girders together at right angles. Can you build a cube shape with more strips of card?

Here are two challenges to try with your friends:

Challenge 1
Use the card strips and paper fasteners to build a 50 cm-high tower. Test to see if it will support a 100g mass.

Challenge 2
Build a card girder bridge to span a distance of 60 cm. Visit a library and look at books about bridges. It may be useful to use triangular shapes in your construction. Sketch your ideas on paper before you start constructing. Will your bridge support a 100 g mass at its centre? What about 200 g?

Testing metals

YOU WILL NEED

some samples of different metals, such as aluminium, steel, lead, iron, copper, zinc and brass.

a bar magnet
a bowl of water
wire cutters

Carry out these tests on your metal samples. Put your results on a chart like the one shown.

Test 1 Write down the colour of each metal.

Test 2 Describe how each metal feels when you touch it with your fingers.

Test 3 Can you bend each metal using your fingers?

Test 4 Try to cut each metal using wire cutters. Does each one cut easily?

Test 5 What happens when you place the metal samples in a bowl of water? Do they float or sink?

Test 6 What happens when you put a bar magnet next to the metal samples?

Test 7 Think of a way to compare the hardness of each metal.

METAL	COLOUR	FEEL	DOES IT BEND?	CAN IT BE CUT?	FLOAT OR SINK?	MAGNETIC	HARDNESS
Aluminium							
Steel							

Conducting heat

a plastic spoon
a wooden spoon
a metal spoon
a saucepan of water
a candle
3 small wooden beads
a box of matches

● **YOU WILL NEED THE HELP OF AN ADULT**

1. Ask an adult to light a candle and melt some of the wax. Use the melting wax to fix a wooden bead to the end of each spoon.

2. Ask an adult to boil some water in a saucepan. Remove the pan from the cooker.

3. Carefully stand the three spoons in the hot water. Watch what happens to the wooden beads. Which bead falls off first? Why do you think it is the first bead to fall? Which spoon conducts heat the best? Which spoon would you use to stir hot soup cooking in a saucepan and why?

ABOVE
These pyramids, near Cairo in Egypt, were built from huge limestone blocks.

Cement and concrete

Cement is a fine grey powder, which is sometimes known as the builder's glue. When the powder is mixed with water it is used to make things stick together. Without cement we would be unable to bind stones or bricks together. The buildings that we see around us might never have been built. The ancient Egyptians used a cement which contained a substance called gypsum for building their pyramids. The world's largest pyramid, near Cairo in Egypt, was built from over two million blocks of limestone. It is still one of the largest structures in the world.

Greek and Roman builders used a cement called Pozzolana, made from burnt lime, sand and volcanic ash. The Romans also discovered that this cement, when combined with gravel and water, dried to form a hard, rock-like material. This material was used, in the third century, to construct the Colosseum which still stands in the centre of modern Rome. It is a huge building, seating around 45,000 people. It was used for gladiator fights and contests with wild animals.

Pozzolana cement was not improved on until 1756. In that year John Smeaton needed a cement which would withstand weathering from the sea so that he could re-build the Eddystone lighthouse off the Devon coast in England. He experimented with powdered limestone and clay and discovered a product which was better than Pozzolana cement. In 1824 John Aspdin developed Portland cement. The raw materials for this are either chalk and clay or limestone and shale.

They are heated up to 1400° C in a kiln to form lumps of cement called clinker. When the clinker is ground with gypsum it forms Portland cement powder. This is still one of the commonest types of cement in use today. It is usually made near the quarries which supply the raw materials.

LEFT Construction workers laying concrete foundations. Cement is an important ingredient of concrete.

Using cement

1. Cover your working surface with a sheet of
   polythene. Form the plasticine into some
   simple shapes. Use the rolling pin to help you
   and place the shapes on the wooden board.

2. Put 2 spoonfuls of clean water into a plastic
   container. Add 7 spoonfuls of cement powder.
   Mix the cement and water to form a paste.
   Add a spoonful of water, if necessary, to make
   the paste slightly runny.

3. Pour the cement into the plasticine moulds.
   Leave the cement until it hardens.

4. Carefully remove the plasticine. Notice that
   the material you have made is quite easily
   broken.

Cement is made up of crystals. These are hard particles, each with a definite shape. When water is added to the dry cement powder, new crystals start to grow, forming a solid material. When cement is hard it is said to be 'cured'. Builders sometimes add special materials, called accelerators, to speed up the hardening process. Freezing weather can prevent the hardening process taking place. Ice forming in the wet material stops the crystals linking together.

Concrete is a very useful building material because it can do many different jobs. It is a mixture of three things: cement, aggregate (a substance to make the concrete bulky) and water. The aggregate is often gravel, sand or crushed stone. Sometimes other materials, such as crushed brick or iron ore, are used if very light or tough concrete is needed. The water used in the mixture must not contain any impurities that will affect the cement. In most cases the water used is pure enough for drinking. Engineers test samples of the concrete before building starts, to check that the aggregate and water are suitable.

Concrete is used in a whole range of building tasks, including providing the foundations for houses, for floor surfaces and in building skyscrapers, bridges, tunnels and dams. Concrete is not easily crushed or damaged by the weather or chemicals and it is fire-proof.

LEFT The Grand Coulee Dam in the USA is one of the world's largest concrete structures.

Make a concrete garden ornament

cement
sand
gravel or very
small stones
plasticine
a wooden board
Vaseline
a small trowel

a jug of water
tin cans
newspaper
a sheet of polythene
a knife
a rolling pin
a large old bowl

● **WEAR GLOVES AND GOGGLES AND BE CAREFUL NOT TO BREATHE IN ANY CEMENT POWDER**

● **YOU WILL NEED AN ADULT TO HELP YOU**

1. Cover your working surface with newspaper. Roll out the plasticine until it is flat and about 0.5 cm thick. Cut it into strips about 3 cm wide. Place these strips on the wooden board so that they form a mould in the shape of an animal, such as a cat.

2. When making concrete follow the safety precautions on the packet. Wear gloves to protect your hands. Measure out three cans of gravel, two cans of sand and one can of cement powder. Put these materials together in a large bowl and use the trowel to mix them well. Add a little water and continue to stir until you have a stiff mixture.

3. Smear the inside of your plasticine mould with Vaseline. Pour the concrete into the mould. Tap the concrete surface with the trowel to push out any air bubbles.
Cover your animal shape with a polythene sheet and leave it for a few days to harden. Then carefully remove the plasticine from your finished concrete animal.

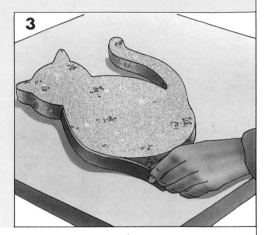

Although concrete is a strong material, it still does not have enough strength for certain building jobs. By placing steel rods inside the concrete before it hardens it can be made very much stronger. This type of concrete, which can withstand squashing and stretching, is known as reinforced concrete. To make an even stronger material engineers have developed pre-stressed concrete. Here the steel rods or cables are stretched before the concrete hardens.

BELOW
The Sydney Opera House in Australia is an imaginative concrete building.

Make a model reinforced concrete beam bridge

1. Cover your working surface with a sheet of polythene. Cut the wood into two strips that are 40 cm long and two that are 10 cm long. Use them to make a mould. Tie some string tightly around the mould. Lightly smear the inside of the mould with Vaseline.

2. When making concrete wear gloves and goggles and ask an adult to help you. Using a large tin can measure out three cans of gravel, two cans of sand and one can of cement powder. Mix these materials together in a bowl. Stir in a little water. Use the trowel to mix the materials. The mixture should be quite stiff. Add more water if necessary.

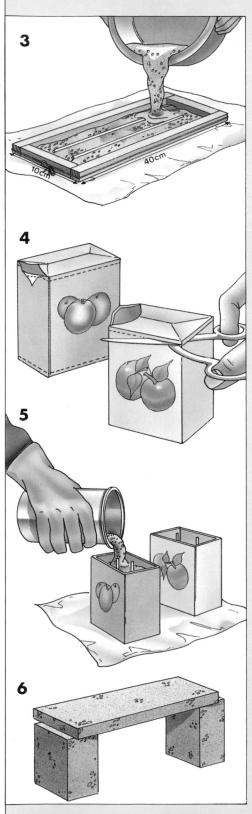

3. Pour some of the concrete into the mould until it is about half full.

   Use the wire cutters to cut two lengths of wire each about 38 cm long. Place these wires on the wet concrete. Add more concrete to the mould. It should be level with the top of the wood. Tap the concrete with a piece of wood to push out any air bubbles. Leave the reinforced concrete beam to harden. When it is hard remove the wooden mould.

4. Use scissors to remove the top and bottom sections from the cardboard fruit juice containers.

5. Make some concrete. Use the same method as before. Smear the insides of both cardboard containers with Vaseline. Pour concrete into each container.

   Cut some short lengths of wire and place them vertically in the concrete. Add more concrete until the containers are full. Leave to harden. Remove the reinforced concrete from the containers.

6. Place your reinforced concrete beam on the two supports. How could you test the strength of your beam bridge?

Look out for beam bridges. They are often built, using concrete and steel, to cross motorways.

Bricks and mortar

Bricks, made from clay, have been used in construction for thousands of years. Clay is cheap and plentiful and is therefore an ideal material for making building blocks. Bricks are made in a variety of shapes and sizes but are usually easy to lift and fit comfortably into one's hand. In many countries bricks are now produced by machines which squeeze the clay into strips. These strips are then cut into standard brick sizes. The bricks are dried and baked or fired in a kiln at 1,000° C. This process produces the hard brick material which we find in many buildings around us.

Bricklayers use mortar to join the bricks together. Mortar is often made by mixing cement, lime, sand and water. The mortar mixture needs to stick to the bricks, to be strong and to be easy for the bricklayer to use. Try to watch how a bricklayer uses a trowel to construct a wall from bricks and mortar.

Look at the walls of some brick built houses. You will see that the bricks have been laid in a pattern. This pattern, called the bond, gives the wall strength and makes it look attractive.

ABOVE Look for patterns in brick walls.

Bricks and water

2 large plastic bowls
six house bricks
a bucket of water
a polythene sheet
cardboard
aluminium foil
scissors

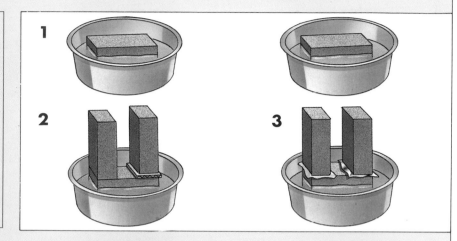

1. Place a brick in each bowl. Carefully pour water around the bricks. The level of water should reach halfway up the bricks as shown.

2. Place one brick vertically on top of the brick in bowl 1. Place a second brick vertically on the other end of the brick. Cut a piece of cardboard and place it between the horizontal brick and the second vertical brick as shown.

3. Make a similar arrangement with the second bowl. Use a layer of polythene with one brick and a layer of aluminium foil with the second.

4. Leave the bricks for half an hour. Look at them closely. Has anything happened to the top bricks? What happens after one hour? What happens after a day?

Water can enter a building by creeping up the brick walls from ground level. To prevent this, builders insert a damp-proof layer near the base of a building. The material used for this layer needs to be non-porous, strong and long-lasting. Bitumen and polythene sheeting are often used. Look at the brick walls of some buildings. Can you see the thin damp-proof layer near the base of the building?

Glass

Glass is a strong transparent material. It comes in a range of types and has many uses in building. In 1959, a British glass manufacturer called Pilkington invented and started to make Float glass. The name of the glass comes from the method by which molten glass is floated on a perfectly flat surface of molten tin. The glass is gradually cooled, whilst it is still floating, and finally forms perfectly flat, polished sheets of glass. The production of Float glass revolutionized the manufacture of glass for use in the windows of houses, hotels, offices, shops and other buildings.

BELOW
Glass helps to make many modern buildings look attractive.

Toughened glass, five times stronger than ordinary glass, is used where extra safety is required, such as internal doors, shower screens and in schools. Laminated glass, made from a sandwich of plastic between two sheets of clear glass, gives greater security than toughened glass. It is used to deter thieves in banks, jewellers and some private houses. The plastic layer holds the glass together even when the outer glass layers are shattered. Wired glass is used in buildings where there are fire risks. Wire mesh is sandwiched between two sheets of glass. If the glass cracks in a fire the pieces are held in place by the wire. This prevents injury by falling glass and reduces the spread of flames.

BELOW
Many chapels and churches have stained glass windows.

RIGHT The big glass windows of this skyscraper will let a lot of light into the rooms inside.

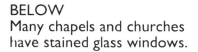

The first glass was produced in the Eastern Mediterranean about 4000 BC. Glass was probably first made in Britain during the time of the Roman Empire. The Romans' glass-making ideas spread throughout Europe. By the 16th century the main product of European glassmakers was window glass.

The raw materials used to make glass - sand, soda ash and limestone - are readily available and glass is, therefore, relatively cheap to produce. Look for examples of patterned and stained glass windows in churches, cathedrals and elsewhere.

Timber

Timber is strong, light and easily cut and shaped. It is attractive to look at and can be painted, varnished and treated with preservatives to make it very long-lasting. In some parts of the world, where a lot of trees grow, entire houses are built of wood. The log cabins of Scandinavia, Canada and the USA have walls built from the trunks and branches of trees. The roofs are also made from timber.

Timber frames, where timbers are jointed together, have been used for centuries to build barns, churches and cottages. You will still find buildings, some dating back to the 13th century, where the timber frame is clearly visible. The frame provides a rigid skeleton that can be filled in with material such as wattle and daub, plaster or brick. In many cases the timber used is oak, which is hard and very strong.

BELOW Timber is used for building houses, like these in Colorado, USA.

Many modern houses are built using timber frameworks. The roof timbers, for example, are assembled in factories and then transported to the building sites. These frameworks are quickly placed in position and covered by roofing material. Timber is also widely used to make doors and door frames, floorboards, joists, window frames and stairs.

RIGHT
The roofs of modern houses often have timber frameworks.

The timber used in building comes from the softwood and hardwood forests of the world. The trees are cut down using power chain saws. When the branches have been removed the trees are cut into logs and transported to sawmills. Once in the sawmills, the logs are sawn up into boards and planks. Large sawmills are now controlled by computers. They can convert thousands of logs into timber, for use by builders, within one day. Before the timber can be used it has to be dried or seasoned. This is because the newly-sawn timber contains a lot of moisture. Most timber is seasoned in special kilns where the water is carefully taken out. Once this is done the timber is packaged and sent, by sea and land, to where it is needed.

Timber is used in vast quantities and it is important, therefore, that we look after the forests of the world. New forest areas need to be created and we must consider carefully the types of timber we use for particular jobs.

Build a timber-framed model house

1. Use your ruler and pencil to draw vertical lines at 3 cm intervals on a sheet of thin card. Draw horizontal lines at 3 cm intervals as well. Now draw diagonal lines as shown. Cut out the triangles you have drawn. Keep them in a plastic container until they are needed.

2. Mark out 60 cm on a length of 1 cm square wood. With an adult present, use the hacksaw to cut through the wood, on top of the bench hook. Repeat this so that you have four lengths of wood each measuring 60 cm and eight lengths of wood each measuring 30 cm.

3. Take a 60 cm length of wood and place it at right angles to a 30 cm length. Apply some

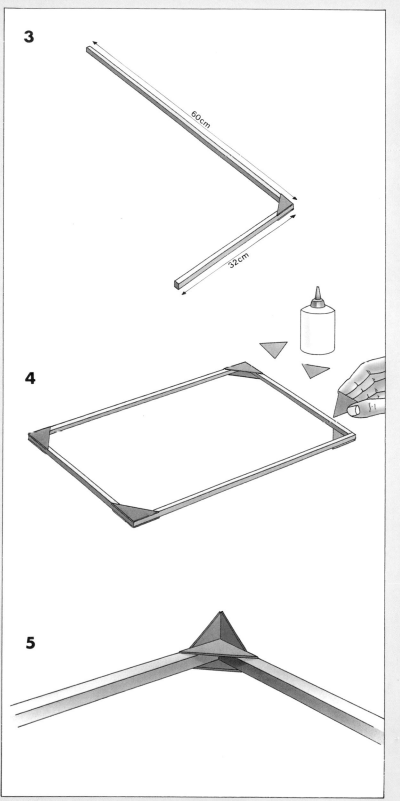

PVA glue to one side of a card triangle and position it over the corner. Leave it to dry. Repeat this so that you have a rectangle measuring 60 cm by 32 cm. Carefully turn this rectangle over and glue a card triangle to the other side of each corner. Leave the rectangle to set.

4. Make a further rectangle exactly the same size as the first. Use eight card triangles and PVA glue, as before, to make the joints.

5. Take two card triangles and glue them, as shown, to one corner of the 60 cm by 32 cm rectangle. Glue card triangles to each of the other corners. Leave them to set. Repeat this with the second rectangle that you have already made.

6. Glue the four 30 cm uprights in position to form a box structure. Glue lollipop sticks across each corner, as shown.

7. Cut four lengths of wood measuring 10 cm and four lengths measuring 16 cm. Use the glue and card triangles to make two window frames as shown.

8. Use the same method to make a further two window frames as shown. Start by cutting four lengths of wood measuring 15 cm long and four lengths of wood each measuring 12 cm.

9. Cut two lengths of wood each measuring 15 cm and two measuring 8 cm long. Construct the framework for the front door of your house, as shown.

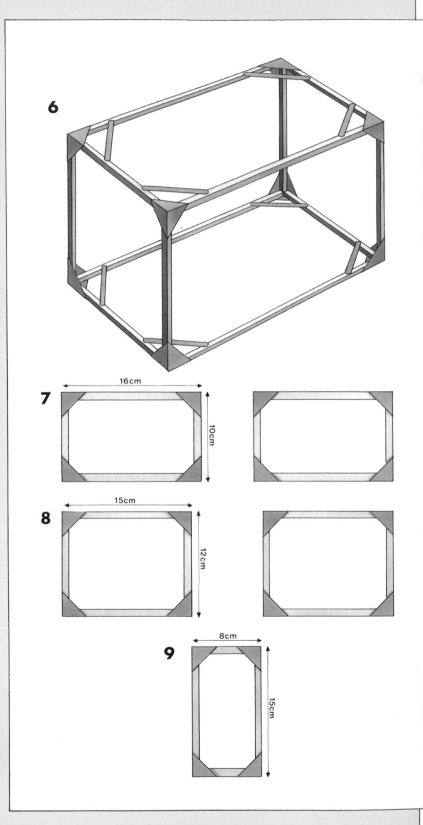

6

7 16 cm 10 cm

8 15 cm 12 cm

9 8 cm 15 cm

0

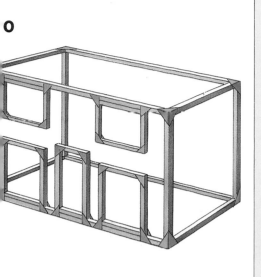

1

2

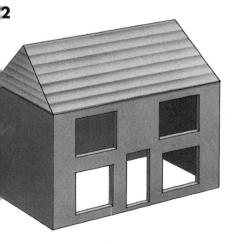

10. Use card triangles and glue to fix the window frames and door frame to the front of your house. If you wish, make window frames for the sides and rear of the house. Make a rear exit to the house. Perhaps you could design and build a front porch.

11. To make the roof, first cut two lengths of wood measuring 30 cm and a further six lengths measuring 29 cm each. Take a 30 cm length and a 29 cm length of wood and fix them together as shown. Repeat this using another 30 cm length and a 29 cm length. Cut a 58 cm length of wood and fix it to the two right angles you have just constructed. Cut two pieces of thick cardboard each measuring 60 cm by 30 cm. Glue these pieces to the wooden framework. Glue the four remaining 29 cm lengths of wood to the inside of the cardboard. Cut two triangular pieces of cardboard, as shown, and glue these to the ends of the roof. The roof should now fit on top of the house framework.

12. Cover the framework of your house with cardboard. Remember to leave spaces for the windows and doors! How could you decorate the outside walls to look like bricks or stones? How could you make the roof look as if it is tiled?

Roofs

The roof of a building has to resist the heat of the sun and the force of the wind, and protect it from pouring rain and snow. To protect the people inside a building from the weather, the material used for the roof covering has to be chosen carefully. An architect will consider the weather conditions that the building will have to face, the natural materials available in the area and whether the covering material blends in with the surroundings. Most important, perhaps, is that the material needs to be hard-wearing, reliable and to last for a long time. Nobody wants to replace a roof within months.

Many buildings, especially those in northern Europe and North America, have steeply sloping roofs which allow rain-water to run off and snow to slip off easily. In other areas of the world, where snow and rain are less frequent, the roofs can be much flatter.

Many types of roof covering materials are now used. Some have been in use for centuries. Thatching, using long straw or wheat reed, has been used for hundreds of years. Clay and slate tiles are used in some areas. Both are non-flammable and last for a long time.

LEFT
Thatch is an attractive and insulating roof covering.

Coloured, interlocking concrete tiles are often used on modern roofs. Cedar wood shingles, which are light in weight, are popular in the USA and Canada. Lead has been used to cover important buildings such as churches and cathedrals. Corrugated iron provides a cheap roofing material. Flat roofs are often covered with bitumen felt and then coated with small chips of rock. Steel sheets, specially coated to prevent rusting, are used to cover modern farming and industrial buildings. All roofing materials will deteriorate with age. Careful maintenance prevents the whole roof having to be replaced.

BELOW
The unusual roof of the Olympic Stadium in Munich, Germany.

For the 1972 Olympic Games an eye-catching stadium was designed and built in Munich, Germany. This remarkable structure has a roof made from acrylic glass plates within a network of steel cables. The plates are 3 m square and just 4 mm thick. This roof, which resembles a cobweb, is designed to be self-cleaning. Rain and snow remove any grime which settles on it. Steel masts, anchored by steel cables, support the roof. The 78,000 spectators inside this tent-like stadium can watch events without the annoyance of pillars to spoil the view.

Look at the roofing materials used in the area around your home. Are they all of the same type or can you identify different materials?

Stonework

Stone is a hardwearing and attractive building material. Many of the world's great structures are built of stone. The Incas built the city of Machu Picchu high in the mountains of South America, using large blocks of stone and only the simplest of tools. Stonehenge, in southern England, was constructed using blocks of stone each weighing up to 40 tonnes. The Chinese used stone to build the 2,250 km-long Great Wall of China. Magnificent churches, castles and cathedrals have been built, using stone, in many parts of the world. These structures, along with the buildings of ancient civilizations, can still be seen today and will be admired in the future. They show the value of stone as a building material.

Before the development of canals and rail networks, locally obtained materials were used for building. To construct a house the builder would have to use stones which were available in the local area. These stones are formed from three main types of rock: igneous rocks, sedimentary rocks and metamorphic rocks.

Igneous rocks are formed by the cooling of molten rock, known as magma. Granite is an igneous rock. It is very hard and is sometimes used in bridges and for kerbstones.

LEFT
The Great Wall of China is an ancient structure made from stone. It was built in the 3rd century BC.

Sedimentary rocks are formed by the breakdown and wearing away of rocks, over millions of years, by the weather, rivers and the seas. Within this group are sandstones and limestones. Limestone is made of tiny shells and calcareous (containing limestone) skeletons that were deposited under the seas.

ABOVE Marble is a hard rock that is sometimes used in building, and sculptures.

Metamorphic rocks have undergone a metamorphosis (change) because of heat and or pressure, movement or chemicals. Originally they may have been igneous or sedimentary rocks. Slate and marble are examples of metamorphic stones used in building. Slate is formed from compressed clay. Marble is produced from limestone that has undergone change by heat and pressure.

Stones are obtained from quarries, often by blasting using explosives, and then they are cut and polished to suit the needs of customers. Today natural stone is expensive and so many builders use artificial stones made from cement and crushed natural stone.

TYPE OF BUILDING	STONE	COLOUR	HOW THE STONES ARE USED

Look at buildings in your town. Keep a chart like the one on the left. Make sketches of some of the buildings. Show where stone has been used as a building material.

LEFT
Painting brickwork helps to protect it from the effects of the weather.

Weathering

The weather can cause building materials to change colour, to crumble, to decay and sometimes to collapse. Architects, engineers and builders have to consider the effects of weather conditions on the materials they decide to use.

High structures, perhaps with a steel framework, need to resist the forces of strong winds. Often, the framework includes a bracing system which makes it more rigid. In some parts of the world the buildings must be able to resist earthquakes. Tall steel frameworks, which sway but do not collapse, have survived a number of earthquakes. Wooden or reinforced concrete beams built into the walls of buildings have also been shown to resist earth tremors.

Wood is easily damaged by various insects and by fungi. Dry rot starts inside buildings where the conditions are damp. The fungus attacks wood and can pass through plaster and even brick to affect the whole building eventually. Wet rot attacks wet timber both inside and outside buildings. It commonly affects windowsills, door frames and fenceposts. To reduce the risk of dry rot, wet rot and insect attack, buildings have to be kept free of damp and the timber should be treated with preservatives such as creosote. Paint and varnishes protect wood by forming a barrier against the effects of the weather. They need to be flexible and allow for the shrinking and swelling of the wood. Otherwise cracks will appear in the paintwork allowing water and fungi to attack the wood.

Metals react with air. They are said to corrode. Rusting is the name given to the corrosion of iron or steel. When iron or steel is used as a building material then rusting can cause serious problems. Reinforced concrete will crack if the steel inside it rusts. This is because the steel increases in volume when it rusts, so forcing the concrete to crack. One way to prevent rusting is to coat the iron or steel with a waterproof barrier such as paint or zinc.

LEFT
This rusty door hinge will need to be replaced.

Stop iron from rusting

YOU WILL NEED

4 clear plastic cups
4 iron nails
grease
oil paint and brush
tap water

1. Fill three of the cups with water. Cover one nail with grease and one with paint. Place a nail in each cup as shown.

2. Leave the nails for three days. Look carefully to see what is happening to the nails. Look again after one week. What changes do you see?

3. Set up the experiment again and try putting the cups and nails in a different place, such as in a cupboard, or outside. Do the changes take place more quickly or slowly? Where do you notice the changes taking place more quickly?

Look at the buildings near your home and school. How many objects can you see that have rusted?

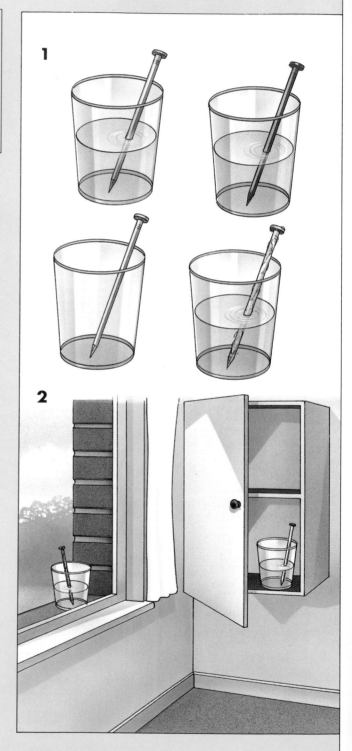

Plaster and plasterboard

Plastering is a building craft which was developed thousands of years ago by the Egyptians, Greeks and Romans. In the late 13th century the 'wattle and daub' technique was developed, using a plaster of clay or dung. Decorative plasterwork, in the form of mouldings and complicated designs, was introduced in the 15th century. The plasterers used a material called stucco, made from a mixture of lime and sand. Many of these intricate designs can still be seen on the ceilings and walls of palaces and other grand buildings.

Today a plaster finish is applied to the walls and ceilings of houses to cover the brickwork or wooden joists and provide a smooth surface. The plaster used needs to be hard, but not brittle, when dry. It needs to set quite quickly, but not shrink or crack as it dries out. Plasters made from a naturally-occurring substance called gypsum are often used. Gypsum-based plasters are easy to work with, set quickly and produce a smooth finish.

ABOVE
Beautiful plasterwork on the outside of a house in San Francisco, USA.

Large plasterboards, ready prepared by sandwiching plaster between two sheets of paper, are now commonly used by builders. They improve insulation and speed up the construction process.

Insulation

When we are inside buildings we like to be warm, especially when the temperature outside is very low. Once the building is heated by an open fire or by a central heating system, then we must stop this heat escaping. Heat can escape through the roof, the walls, the windows and the floor. Buildings need to be insulated so that we do not pay too much for our heating costs and so that we do not waste the world's energy resources.

Double or triple glazing, where a layer of air is trapped between two or three surfaces of glass, can reduce the heat lost through windows considerably. The cavity walls of modern houses, which have a gap between the outer and inner walls, prevent heat being wasted. Insulating materials have been developed that help keep heat inside buildings. These include mineral wool and fibreglass. The use of insulation blocks for the inner walls, and the insertion of an insulating material in the cavity, can reduce heat loss even further. Householders are now advised to insulate the roof area (the loft) of their homes with insulating materials. These materials trap air, which is a good insulator, and stop a lot of the heat from being lost through the roof.

Carpets, fitted with underlay, help to prevent heat loss through floors. Draught excluders and porches with doors can be used to prevent warm air escaping. In Canada and the USA some new buildings are so well insulated that they need little internal heating.

BELOW Insulating the loft area of a house stops heat escaping through the roof.

Saving heat

YOU WILL NEED

a large empty plastic
ice-cream container
an empty drinks can
a thermometer
(0-110°C)
hot water
a measuring jug

insulating materials
(polystyrene, cotton
wool, crumpled paper,
sawdust)
thick paper or card
a watch or stop-clock
graph paper

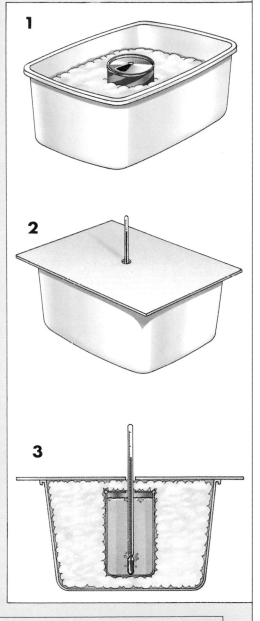

1. Place one of the insulating materials inside the ice-cream container. Fill a drinks can with hot water and place the can on top of the insulating material. Pack more insulating material around the can as shown. Make a card lid to fit over the container. Put a thermometer, through a hole in the card, into the can of hot water.

2. Read the temperature every five minutes and write your results on a table like the one shown.
Try the experiment again with different insulating materials.

MATERIAL	TEMPERATURE					
	START	5 MINS	10 MINS	15 MINS	20 MINS	25 MINS

Plastics and the future

Plastics have a number of uses in the construction industry. A thermoplastic called polyvinyl chloride (PVC) can be made in a range of forms from pliable (soft) to rigid. Soft forms of PVC are used to cover electric wires. Rigid PVC is used to make guttering, drainpipes, roofing sheets, electrical fittings and piping for use in plumbing. Some plastics are good insulating materials. Rigid plastic is now also used to make window and door frames, doors and skirting boards.

Some manufacturers in the USA suggest that thermoplastics can replace many of the building materials in use today. It may be that some houses in the future will be constructed from plastic modules. These modules will be mass-produced in factories and assembled on site. Such houses will need to be energy-saving and so may use a recent invention - low cost solar roof tiles. These tiles replace normal roofing tiles and can convert the sun's rays into electricity for use in the house.

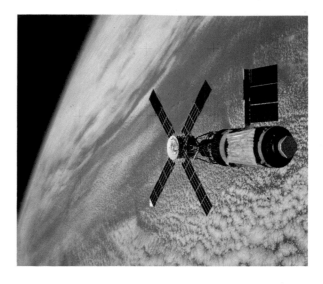

ABOVE New materials will be developed for use in space and on Earth.

When plastic resin and glass fibres are combined they form a composite material called glass-reinforced plastic. This material is light but strong. It has recently been used in the building of the world's first bridge made entirely out of composite materials. This 120 m bridge spans the River Tay in Scotland. The engineers involved in this project believe that glass fibre reinforced plastic could be used instead of aluminium, steel and concrete in many buildings. They plan to construct office blocks and houses using similar all-composite materials.

Topic Web

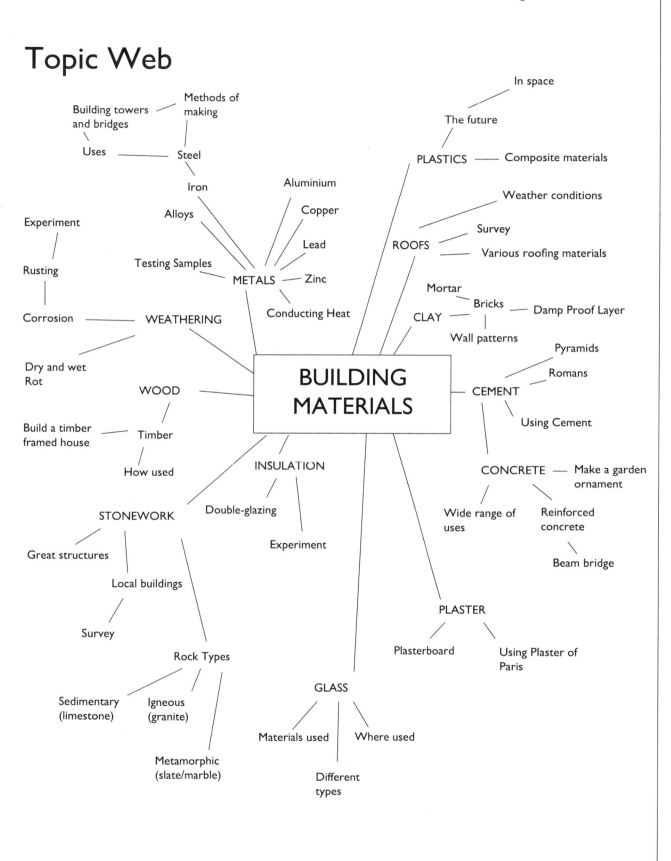

Glossary

Alloy
A mixture of two or more metals, or a metal with another substance.

Architect
Someone who designs and plans buildings.

Bitumen
A black substance obtained from tar.

Cladding
Material which covers the outside of a building.

Coke
Fuel made from coal that has been heated to a high temperature to remove the gases.

Conduct
To carry electricity.

Creosote
An oily liquid obtained from tar.

Foundations
The base of a building or structure, usually below ground, which has to carry the weight of the building.

Gypsum
A natural material which is a form of calcium sulphate.

Hardwood
Timber produced from deciduous trees.

Insulation
Filling a space with a material that does not allow heat.

Joists
Lengths of wood or metal used to support ceilings, floors or other structures.

Manganese
A brittle, greyish-white metal.

Mass
The amount of matter in an object. Units of mass are grams, kilograms and tonnes. Mass is often confused with weight which is a measure of the force of gravity on an object.

Mastic asphalt
A black, sticky material which is similar to tar.

Modules
Self-contained units.

Molten
In a liquid form.

Mould
A shape into which a liquid substance is poured so that it takes on the same shape when it has set.

Nomadic
People who do not have fixed homes, but wander from place to place.

Non-porous
Not able to absorb air or liquid.

Ore
A rock or mineral from which metals can be extracted.

Resin
A substance used in the plastics industry.

Shingles
Wooden slabs or boards.

Solar
To do with the sun.

Thermoplastic
A plastic which softens when heated and hardens when cooled.

Transparent
Able to be seen through.

Wattle and daub
A method of building by interweaving twigs or branches and plastering them with clay, mud or straw and dung.

Books to read

Encyclopaedia of Modern Technology edited by D Blackburn and G Holister (Hutchinson, 1987)

Young Engineer on the Road by M Dixon (Wayland, 1983)

How They Were Built by D J Brown (Kingfisher Books, 1991)

Structures by M Dixon (Wayland, 1990)

Great Buildings by P Bagenal and J Meades (Tiger Books International, 1990)

How Things Are Built by H Edam (Usborne, 1989)

Places to visit

Science Museum
Exhibition Road
South Kensington
London

Weald and Downland Open Air Museum
Singleton
Chichester
Sussex

The Building Centre
26 Stove Street
London WC1E 7BT

Llechweld Slate Caverns
Blaenau Ffestiniog
Gwynedd
Wales

Blue Circle Heritage Centre
The Creek
Northfleet
Kent

Young Designers Centre
Design Centre
28 Haymarket
London SW1

The Building Innovation Gallery
The Building Centre
113-115 Portland Street
Manchester M1 6FB

Hartley Wood Glass Experience
Portobello Lane
Monkwearmouth
Sunderland

Organizations to contact.

Australia

Pilkington (Australia) Ltd
Product Information Centre
7th Floor,
420 St Kilda Road
Melbourne
Victoria 3004

Canada

Contact your local Visitors and Convention Bureau for information about your area.

New Zealand

Ministry of Forestry
P O Box 39
Auckland 1

Remember to send a stamped addressed envelope with your enquiry.

Index